T0304906

L
V
O
E.

Volume II

Also by Atticus

Spark
LVOE.
The Truth About Magic
The Dark Between Stars
Love Her Wild

LVOE.

Volume II

ATTICUS

HEADLINE

First published in 2024 by
HEADLINE PUBLISHING GROUP

First published in the US in 2024 by
Andrews McMeel Publishing
a division of Andrews McMeel Universal
1130 Walnut Street, Kansas City, Missouri 64106
www.andrewsmcmeel.com

1

Illustrations by Marissa Campeau @_mcampeau

Cataloguing in Publication Data is available from the British Library

Hardback ISBN 978 1 4722 9386 2

Offset in 12.12/16.16 pt Baskerville URW by Jouve (UK), Milton Keynes

Printed and bound in China by C&C Offset Printing Co., Ltd.

Headline's policy is to use papers that are natural, renewable and recyclable
products and made from wood grown in well-managed forests and other
controlled sources. The logging and manufacturing processes are expected
to conform to the environmental regulations of the country of origin.

HEADLINE PUBLISHING GROUP
An Hachette UK Company
Carmelite House
50 Victoria Embankment
London EC4Y 0DZ

www.headline.co.uk
www.hachette.co.uk

About the title, LVOE.

A few years ago, I designed an engagement ring for my wife. It had two oval stones placed on a single gold band that together made an imperfect heart. I called it Coeur Parfait, *which in French means* perfect heart, *for to me love has always been two imperfect things coming together to make something beautiful. That's the reason I named this book* LVOE, *because even though love is imperfect, we all still can see the beauty.*

xx
Atticus

I wrote this book on stolen time,
at parties, at work,
on trains and planes—
and I stole it all for you.

—Atticus

CHAPTERS

*"I've dreamt in my life dreams that have stayed
with me ever after, and changed my ideas:
they've gone through and through me, like wine
through water, and altered the colour of my mind."*

–Emily Brontë, excerpt from Wuthering Heights

To my growing family,
for filling my heart with a love
I never imagined could be mine.

1.

HER

*"I love her and that's the beginning
and end of everything."*

–F. Scott Fitzgerald

Her soul was a garden
blooming with hope
and with each new day
she tended to its weeds and wounds
bringing it ever slowly
back to life.

Some days
she was the flower
some days she was the storm
but always she was the meadow
and it is the meadow that I love.

Her eyes held all those secrets
that her heart was too shy to tell.

He was so wild and gentle all at once
like wandering into a storm
and finding only silence
and she loved that about him
he was a constant rebellion against the boring and the ordinary
forever unexpected
and she let herself—
for this moment of her youth—
surrender into his winds.

♥

Her life was a tapestry
woven together with stories
of joy and sadness
moments of pain but also hope—
and within those threads of life
she created herself
in every stitch of colored string.

She was my muse.
an endless fountain of
beautiful colors and words—
and all she ever did
was exist
as so effortlessly herself.

She never saw the beautiful girl
who everybody else seemed to see
all she saw were the scars and imperfections
screaming back at her in the mirror
that she would never be enough
that she could never be beautiful—
and she always wondered
why the whole world
would lie to her
and only this mirror
tell the truth.

Those eyes
lapped against the shores of my soul
like the ocean does at dawn
in the peaceful blue way of a new morning
and I fell for those eyes
and the calm dawns I saw within.

My love for her was forever a constellation
guiding me ever on
through the rocky roads of life.

♥

Into his arms
she fell
into the warming waters of belonging
unjudged and unconditional
it was soaking safely there in those arms
where she found home.

SHE LOVED ME
LONG BEFORE I LOVED MYSELF
FOR INSIDE ME
SHE SAW EVERYTHING
I WASN'T YET
BRAVE ENOUGH
TO SEE.

I crave only the truth of you
that deep-down buried truth
that truth you keep hidden from the world
forever so magnificently.

Her heart
was her guide
leading her ever on
toward the life that whispered to her from beyond—
and she followed its beating path
with a smile
knowing everything she ever dreamed of
was just along the way.

A piece of her —
all of her maybe —
missed the dark and wild chaos
of their long-forgotten love.

Her tears were a river
flowing out from her soul
washing away the old stories—
and day by day
her tears began to heal her from within
and the sadness slowly drained
carried off downstream and over the horizon
to that shadowy place
with all the other forgotten things
that once were important
but now
no longer mattered.

Travel is not about escaping ourselves
it's about discovering ourselves from the outside in.

My heart aches for you
always in the dead of night
the thoughts swirl in a storm
of memories and regrets
I try to push them away
but they cling to me like ivy
wrapped so tightly round my soul—
I suffocate for you
and the memories of love gone by.

I saw you in my dreams last night again
you wandered in
a ghost but real
so real I could still feel your warmth
your touch more alive than any touch of day
your lips softer than any kiss awake
I told myself you were a dream
that you were a long time gone now
but my soul whispered to me
that you were real
wandering—somehow—between our worlds.

As the rain falls
on this old moss roof
I am reminded
of our storms together
in that cabin long ago
with the fire burning
and the kettle boiling—
gone are those days
but with me still
the warm and rainy days of you.

There in all the chaos and wonders of new love
she surrendered herself to him
placing her heart and soul
gently into his hands
and crossing her heart
to the wild whims of fate.

The sun set behind her
casting a long shadow into her past
but she didn't look back
not anymore
she walked only forward
on toward the light
away from the darkness of an old life
and on
into the coming of a new day.

2.

LOVE

*"Love is life. All, everything that I understand,
I understand only because I love."*

–Leo Tolstoy

Love is a key
that unlocks
the greatest mysteries of life
revealing all the beauty and wonders
that lie sleeping within us
waking us to all the colors and songs
we held tightly in our hearts as secrets.

LOVE IS THE ALCHEMY OF LIFE—
TRANSFORMING
WATER INTO WINE
HEARTS TO GOLD
AND OUR TWO SOULS INTO MAGIC.

♥

Love is not a place at which to arrive
it's a journey on which to embark
an adventure to begin
on which we will learn
as much about ourselves
as we will about our loves—
and that's the great wonder of it all
it's in all those magic steps along the way.

The greatest mistake in love
is to expect our partners
to be everything for us
that we are not.

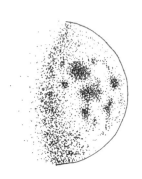

WHEN WE LOVE SOMEONE
WE ARE SAYING TO THEM
"I CHOOSE YOU
I CHOOSE YOU
AND I WILL KEEP CHOOSING YOU
UNTIL THE END OF TIME."

♥

Love
is the art of accepting a person
for exactly who they are
who they were
and who they will one day be.

Love was the music that brought harmony to our lives
and the rhythm that kept us dancing through the hard times—
and we knew as long as we were together
we would never stop dancing
not until the place was closed
the chairs were up
and the rest of the world
had gone home.

ATTICUS

The greatest secret of love
is that the more vulnerable we become
the safer we will be.

♥
35

To love is to feel the warmth of the sun
and the chill of the wind all at once–
it's a grand and miraculous shiver down your spine.

♥

LOVE WAS A SPRING BREEZE

CARRYING WITH IT

THE SWEET FRAGRANCE OF HOPE

THAT WHISPERED TO OUR YOUNG HEARTS

THE PROMISE

OF A NEW TOMORROW.

To love is to surrender
to place your heart into another's hands
while praying to the stars
that they will be more gentle this time.

Love is not about the possessing of something
it's about the sharing of all things—
the sharing of space
the sharing of souls
the sharing of time.

♥

The river of love
flows between each of us
in this universe
connecting us all
to the infinite ocean of existence.

Love is not about hiding who we are
it's about discovering the parts of ourselves
we never knew were there.

When we love someone
we become a mirror
reflecting back
the truth of them
and all the beauty and shadows they possess.

♥

The greatest expression of love
is not in the words you say
it's in the actions you take
day after day
year after year
it's the showing up
that becomes the truth of your love.

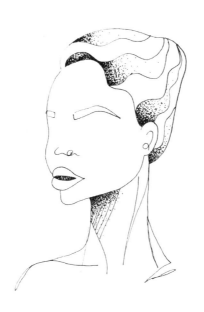

Love is a wondrous thing
a mysterious magic glue
that binds us all together
even when the rest of the world
falls apart.

Love is not always gentle
sometimes it's a wildfire
consuming everything in its path
leaving nothing behind
but smoke and ash
and even then—
when the smoke clears
and the fires fade—
we all still crave its warmth.

♥

Love is the linger of flowers in the air
that stays with us
long after the roses have gone
and petals fallen—
reminding us forever after
of the beauty that once was
and could one day be again.

To love someone
is to see the world through their eyes
to feel their pain
and their pasts
and to hold those little secrets
safely in our hands
as carefully as if
they were our own.

WHEN WE LOVE SOMEONE

WE GIVE THEM THE POWER

TO BREAK US

BUT ALSO

THE CHANCE TO HEAL US

IN A WAY

WE'VE NEVER BEEN HEALED BEFORE.

♥

Love is the poetry of souls
painting our lives with bleeding colors
from the deepest depths of our hearts—
through every kiss, word, and wrinkled page
we write our truth.

♥

To love
is to risk being broken
into a million pieces
and knowing
it is still
worth the risk.

Love is a language
that we all speak differently—
I sing songs to my love
silly songs with made-up lyrics
and no beat
or rhythm
or rhyme
but they all say the same thing
in the same way—
"I love you."

When someone has received
unconditional love in their life
it shows up
in all the little ways they are
how they carry themselves
how they love others—
and how they always know
exactly how they deserve to be loved.

♥

Love whispers to all of us
but not all of us are ready to listen.

If your life is too busy for love then your life is too busy for life.

♥

3.

PEACE

"I like living. I have sometimes been wildly despairing, acutely miserable, racked with sorrow, but through it all I still know quite certainly that just to be alive is a grand thing."

—Agatha Christie, from An Autobiography

POETRY IS MY REFUGE
A SANCTUARY AGAINST THE CHAOS OF LIFE
THAT GIVES ME THE POWER TO SPEAK
WHAT MY HEART CANNOT SAY ALOUD.

♥

Their young love
was a kaleidoscope
of lights and colors
a tangled pastel haze
with no sense of where one soul began
and the other ended
and the universe—
as it always did
with new love—
shone down upon them
in shooting stars.

I saw my first sunset with you
I'd seen them before
but not like this—
you saw colors
I had only dreamed of
colors you can only feel
when you close your eyes and listen
to the warm miracle unfolding before you.

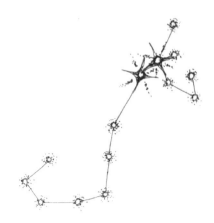

The universe was a mystery to us
and we loved to wonder in its vastness
as we lay in the fields
and chased clouds across the sky—
we were specks on a rock
spinning through the dark of space—
but the grandness of all things
never seemed to matter much
with the smallness
of your hands in mine.

They tell you to be happy, don't they?
But you know
and I know
it's never that easy
is it?

In the grand forest of my soul
there is a place I know
with a meadow
where the sun shines
and the wild roses and bluebonnets bloom
where the long grass waves
in the warm breeze of summer
and in the center
a small tree stands alone
with spring petals blooming brightly year-round—
this is who you are within me
you are for now and always
the warm summer meadow
of my soul.

All nature is a reflection of our souls
the chaos and harmony of its rhythms
are a mirror into the truth of ourselves.

I feel a great peace with you
like a cabin in a storm
where the wild world rages around us
pelting windows with wind and rain
but we are happy
safe and alone
in our own little world
playing games that only we know
drinking wine—
and dancing
to songs about the sun.

Her scars
were not her flaws
they were her story
reminding her forever
of the long journey
that had made her
exactly who she was.

We lay in the tall grass
chasing clouds across the sky
swimming through
those gentle blues
as little fish do in their silver seas—
we had no place to go
but each other's minds
and so we danced in them together
up through our dreams
laughing at the silly things we saw—
magic string castles
and cotton candy creatures—
all alive within the carnivals of our minds
and we'd smile and laugh
tangled up
in each other's youth—
two souls as one
in a magic sugar sea.

I am the storm
and the calm before as well—
never one
without the other—
so if you want me truly
you must take me fully
storms and gentle seas alike.

♥

Don't keep the words caged inside you
they are free things with wings, you see?
Wild creatures
that if kept inside too long
will rattle against the cage
trying to escape—
instead, let them soar away from you
let them fly
and spread their wings into the sun—
for only once you've let them free
can your caged soul too
find its wings.

It took me a lifetime
to learn to be kind to myself
to let go of the judgment
for all my flaws and imperfections—
for now I see the truth of it all
a scared little boy within
fearful and alone
without the love and protectors he yearned for
instead, I give this child
all the love and protection he never had
and slowly and surely
our love heals us both.

As we stumble along
this road of life
I'm glad we walk it together
stumbling forever as one
like two young lovers
walking home from the bar.

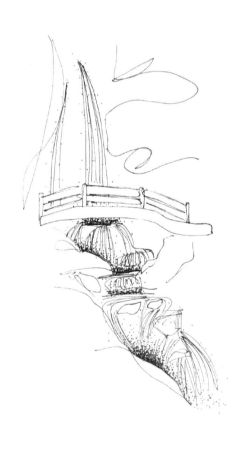

She was light in the darkness
a beacon of hope
for all of us lost in the shadows
and when she left us
so long before her time
the world became a little colder—
but sometimes still
on those darkest and cold nights
when we close our eyes just right
we can all still feel her glow.

All my life
I have believed that I am not enough
not worthy of love or happiness
but then one day I began to listen
to what the universe was whispering to me all along
that we are all perfect here
and that the universe
doesn't create anything
that's not perfectly enough already.

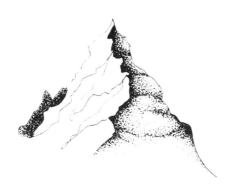

I will be a rock for you, my love
through all the ups and downs
for all the troubles of the world to crash upon—
I will be there for you
steady and unmoving—
even in those wildest storms
I will not budge
for I am a mountain for you
as you have always been for me.

Poetry is about seeing something beautiful
and writing it down
in such a way
that we don't forget the beauty.

♥

WORDS ARE SUCH MEAGER TOOLS
FOR ME TO PAINT
WHAT MY HEART FEELS FOR YOU.

Give me some old friends laughing in the desert
underneath the stars—
and _I_ will show you the meaning
of this wild and precious life.

A well-hidden note
is more powerful
than a bed of roses
but both is always better.

♥

There's something magic
about the ocean
as if it holds
in its glistening folds
all the secrets and memories of the world
and whispers them back to us
one by one
as crashing waves
and raging storms.

♥

I dream of those moments
on the banks of rivers and forests
in the mossy holds of nature
when the world
and all its worries seem to fade
and we find only peace around us
whispering there as a gentle breeze
of what all life is
and why.

Sometimes we say more in a lingered hug
than a long conversation.

All art is a mirror that reflects the world around us
showing us both the light and the dark within us all.

My heart is a meadow
of wildflowers and thorns
and sometimes I forget to remember
that both are me—
and that's okay.

I AM LITTLE PIECES
OF ALL THE PEOPLE
AND ALL THE PLACES
I HAVE EVER KNOWN
AND EACH PIECE
HAS MADE ME A LITTLE BIT MORE
WHO I AM.

♥

4.

HOPE

*"Endure the hardship of the present and
focus on the happiness that is to come."*

–Homer

Hope is a flame
that warms our hearts
even on the coldest nights of doubt—
it lives within us
as a glimmer
leading us forever
out of the dark.

Do not fear this broken heart
let it be a reminder
that you are a human
capable of loving something deeply—
and that is a gift
that many don't possess.

The most important battle
she ever fought
was the fight for herself
to love and accept
exactly who she was.

In the light of love
the darkness of fear and doubt dissolve
and the soul is bathed in the radiant warm rays of hope.

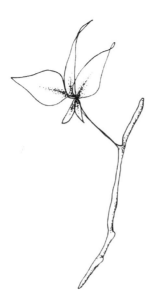

The hardest part of heartbreak
is that it is a journey we must embark on alone
but alone
we will also emerge
stronger, wiser, and reborn.

Sometimes the greatest act of love
is to let love go
to release it into the past
and make space
for a new beginning.

Art is a language of the soul
a canvas that calls to us
throughout the folds of time
through paint, and clay, and song.

There is a great fire
burning within us all
churning with the possibilities of life
and the constant reminder that we are alive
and capable of anything we set our minds to
and if we ever forget that fiery truth
the world will quickly
burn our eyelashes.

She had loved more times than she could count
and each time it hurt a little less than the last
but she wouldn't give up
not while the hope of love still lived within her
for love, she knew
made this strange and wonderful adventure worth living.

♥

So many years
since she had passed
and still
he put the kettle on
just in case
her ghost arrived
in time for tea.

The magic of art
is that it has the power
to turn our pain into poetry.

The sunset was a canvas
carved of pinks and golds
and it warmed our battered souls
healing us
from the inside out
as if for the first time in all our lives
our hearts had been dipped
in that golden honey
they call hope.

There is a beauty in our brokenness
in the way the light seeps in through the cracks
and how the jagged edges of our souls align
to always let the hope inside.

Don't look for someone to make you whole —
look for someone to share your wholeness with

Some people enter our lives
for the sole purpose
of teaching us
exactly who we are not looking for.

Love is a fire that consumes the soul
and leaves behind only ash and whispers
of the ghosts we were before.

The world around us is a perfect reflection
of our innermost thoughts and beliefs
a reminder
that the power to create our reality
lies within the minds of every one of us.

♥

The moon shines to me
in the stillness of the night
a reminder that even in this darkest dark
there will always be light
for those of us who need it most.

All we poets have
is all the world's words before us
and a million different ways to place them
in our never-ending search
to find something beautiful.

She was unafraid to speak her truth
to stand up against the tyranny she saw around her
it was never a choice—
some people are born to fight against the worst of us
for the rest of us.

♥

The hardest part about being sad
is that we lose the ability to see
the beauty in the world around us.

In art
there is no right or wrong
only the courage to believe.

My heart
is a wild and fragile thing
broken apart
a thousand times and more––
and each time it is put back together
it leaves a different picture
of the imperfect puzzle that I am.

Our greatest power
lies not in our ability to control the world
but in our capacity
to control our minds within it.

MY BODY IS A TEMPLE

OF RESILIENCE AND STRENGTH

EACH NEW SCAR

A TESTAMENT

TO MY ABILITY TO ENDURE

A CONSTANT REMINDER

OF WHO I AM

AND WHERE I'M GOING.

For the first time in her life
she began to fall in love
with who she was in this world
every scar
every imperfection
became a unique and beautiful truth
that made her perfect.

A great lesson of life
is that we don't need to change anyone's opinion
we have the power to leave others to their own beliefs
and believe whatever we want to believe
with whoever we want to believe it with—
and that simple truth
will set us free.

Our hearts
so quickly forget
that there just might be
other love stories
waiting for us
out there
somewhere.

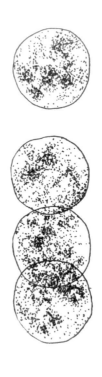

5.

TIME

*Time is
Too Slow for those who Wait,
Too Swift for those who Fear,
Too Long for those who Grieve,
Too Short for those who Rejoice,
But for those who Love,
Time is Eternity.*

—Dr. Henry Van Dyke

Maybe we are all just stories
waiting to be read by someone we love.

Though you are gone now
and far away
your memory lingers on
a nostalgic ghost
haunting me
on rainy days—
but, still, I cherish it and us
and the old ways we were
not in a sad way
or a mad way—
for it is too far and long ago
for that now—
but, still, I will keep these memories and you
with me always
playing in my heart like an old film—
a sepia remembering of long ago.

Do not dream
to change your past
dream instead
to remember
these lessons learned
and find the courage
to change your future.

Let go of yesterday
and the worries within
for the sun rises again each day
to remind us of tomorrow
and the blooming possibilities it holds
a chance to seize the lives
we were born to live
beginning in this moment
beginning on this day.

♥

Anyone
can become a poem
if they are carefully enough observed.

We spend so much of our lives
worrying about the meaning of it all
maybe the answer is simple
to love and be loved
to find a bit of joy
and to embrace this little journey
wherever it may lead.

♥

When we travel
we begin to shed the layers
of who we once were
and become a little bit closer
to who we're meant to be.

This moment is the only truth
we hold in this world—
we must learn to cherish it
for it is here alone
where our entire lives will unfold.

As long as we have our voices
we will always hold the blade
to battle the injustices
and hatreds of our world
we will hold the power
to make a difference
and stand up for what we know is right
and it always starts
with that mighty sword—our voice.

We cannot hope to change the past
we can only hope to change the way we hold it—
learn to honor the stories
and the histories
that have made us who we are
good and bad
only then can we slowly become
those wonderful people
we are pretty sure we can be.

GROWING IS NOT EASY
AND WE MUST LEARN TO TRUST
THE PAIN GROWTH BRINGS
KEEP EDGING EVER ON
TOWARD TOMORROW
AND THE BETTER US
TOMORROW BRINGS.

The beauty of life
is not in the absence of pain
but the strength we find within
to conquer it.

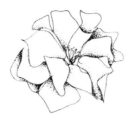

We are all
anxious time travelers
drifting between our pasts
and our futures
forgetting always
the beautiful now
and the perfect present
that could be.

My soul is a garden
and my love is a flower
waiting to one day bloom
dreaming for a chance
to become something beautiful.

Nature is God's muse
allowing poets and artists
to simply observe the world unfolding around them
and paint the truth
of what they see.

Fireflies sparkled
in the autumn grass of summer
blending like paint
into the sky above —
we were two young souls tangled into one
floating there
for a moment of our youth
in the dark
between stars.

Sometimes
the bravest thing
we can do
is to stop searching for love for a moment
and allow our souls
the time and space they need
to heal.

Don't spend too much of your life
pretending to be someone else
or one day
you will wake up
and not remember that beautiful person
you're pretending not to be.

A poet's purpose
is to gently pull
at the fragile yarn of life
and unravel the truths
hidden deep within
the very fabric of us all.

"Leave him,"
the old woman said
"for even if your soul dies this once
it will be born again to live
a thousand times
without him."

She was forever a work in progress
a painting in the making
and every year gone by
was a brushstroke—
another wrinkle, another scar
a reflection of her long-battled journey—
and though she would never be finished
she was in all ways
perfect now.

Nature is the canvas
on which all life is painted
its beauty and magic
the shimmering colors
of the soul who sees it.

I DON'T DREAM TO WRITE
THE GREATEST POEM
THAT HAS EVER BEEN WRITTEN
I ONLY DREAM TO WRITE
A FEW SIMPLE WORDS
THAT COULD MAKE SOMEONE
FOR A MOMENT
FEEL A LITTLE LESS ALONE.

♥

Stay young,
stay brave,
stay wild.

xx Atticus